Elliot Christopher Cowdin

The Presidential Issue and its Effect upon the Business and Prosperity of the Country

Elliot Christopher Cowdin

The Presidential Issue and its Effect upon the Business and Prosperity of the Country

ISBN/EAN: 9783337216122

Printed in Europe, USA, Canada, Australia, Japan

Cover: Foto ©Suzi / pixelio.de

More available books at **www.hansebooks.com**

THE PRESIDENTIAL ISSUE,

AND ITS EFFECT UPON THE BUSINESS AND PROSPERITY OF THE COUNTRY.

SPEECH

OF THE

HON. ELLIOT C. COWDIN,

DELIVERED BEFORE THE

NATIONAL CLUB OF THE CITY OF NEW YORK,

OCTOBER 19, 1868

Published by the NATIONAL CLUB OF THE CITY OF NEW York, in compliance with the following resolution, which was unanimously adopted at the close of the address :

Resolved, That the thanks of the Club be tendered to the Hon. ELLIOT C. COWDIN, for his able and eloquent address, and that a copy of the same be requested for publication.

CLUB HOUSE, New York, Oct. 19, 1868.

THE PRESIDENTIAL ISSUE,

AND ITS EFFECT UPON THE BUSINESS AND PROSPERITY OF THE COUNTRY

SPEECH.

GEN. ANTHON, Chairman of the evening, in a few felicitous and appropriate remarks relative to the important part which the mercantile community had taken in the history of our country, introduced the HON. ELLIOT C. COWDIN, as a representative merchant of New York, who was received with applause, and spoke as follows:

MR. PRESIDENT AND GENTLEMEN: I am not insensible of the honor you have done me by inviting me to address you on the issues of the canvass. Many important considerations press upon our attention, but, as a merchant, I purpose to confine myself to topics relating directly to the Presidential issue, and its effect upon the business and prosperity of the country. In this campaign we are settling the policy of our country not only for the next four years, but, doubtless, for an indefinite period stretching far beyond. As patriots, then, who would so act as to promote the growth and grandeur of the Republic and maintain its integrity and stability, it becomes us to take heed what course we pursue.

Happily, the glorious results of the late war and the measures adopted for the reconstruction of the insurgent States have relieved us, and, we trust, posterity also, from many troublesome questions that were sources of vexation and alarm at every Presidential contest for 30 years previous to the Rebellion.

Negro Slavery is dead beyond the hope of resurrection, and the civil rights of all classes of our population are fixed in the organic law. The union of the States, terribly shattered by one of the greatest convulsions in all history, is restored, and now rests on a basis that cannot be shaken. The Constitution has been vindicated in its original integrity; and it has received new vigor from amendments that not only render all its provisions homogeneous, but have brought it into harmony with the Declaration that proclaims the civil equality of all men.

CONSTITUTIONAL AMENDMENT.

With the Constitutional Amendment known as the XIVth Article, we are all familiar. Two of its sections are seriously assailed by large portions of the Democratic party, and to get rid of these they threaten, so soon as they obtain the power, to erase or disregard the entire article. They are, *first*, that provision which conditionally prevents the holding of certain important offices by such of the insurgents as, previous to the Rebellion, had taken an oath to support the Federal Constitution, and subsequently committed treason by attempting to overthrow the Union; and, *secondly*, that other provision which indirectly regulates the right of suffrage by prescribing a new basis of representation in the Lower House of Congress, and consequently in the Presidential Electoral College. The penalties affixed to the crime of treason by every Government are among the highest known to its laws. In European nations they have ever been of the most sanguinary nature—death under the most ignominious circumstances, and attainder of blood. In our own country these penalties have felt the ameliorating touch of a more liberal civilization; yet even here death may be inflicted.

The history of the world affords no parallel to the magnanimity of the terms of reconstruction tendered to those who, by our civil war, cut off untimely nearly half a million of our sons and brothers, and destroyed thousands of millions of property, entailing poverty and ruin on one-half the Union, and piled up a public debt that imposes on every citizen of the Republic a heavy weight of taxation, and all in the attempt to overthrow the most beneficent Government that ever existed on earth. In punishment of this great crime, not a drop of blood has been shed; scarcely one felon has been even temporarily imprisoned, and only a trifling amount of property has been confiscated; the mass of the Rebels now enjoy to the full every right they forfeited, while a few —a very few—of the leaders who were guilty both of perjury and treason are inhibited from holding positions wherein they might again be tempted to violate their official oaths; and even from this paltry penalty—paltry in view of the crime—they may be relieved, as thousands of them already have been, by a two-thirds vote of Congress. To call this a punishment of treason, and *such* treason, is a ridiculous misnomer; and yet this unprecedented forbearance is unappreciated by these men,—some of the most guilty of whom threaten to kindle anew the flames of civil war, that they may set aside this mild provision of the amended Constitution. But it will stand, and these deluded men will yet learn that it is wiser to accept forgiveness on the terms offered than to provoke the infliction of punishment commensurate with their crimes.

NEGRO SUFFRAGE.

This article further provides that if any State shall deprive any class of its citizens of the right of suffrage—as, for example, because of their color—that State shall not be allowed to count that class in estimating the number of Representatives in Congress to which it shall be entitled. In a word, it declares that if the South regards a portion of its citizens as not fit to wield the ballot, it shall not use their mere numbers as an element of power against a State which treats them as competent to vote.

The Democratic party at the South would deny the male adults of 4,000,000 of their citizens the right to vote, but would themselves elect between thirty and forty members of Congress by virtue of these 4,000,000, and increase to the same extent the weight of that section of the Union in the Presidential Electoral College. Our answer to this is summary. If this class of your citizens ought to be counted as an element of political strength, it ought to be endowed with the elective franchise. If it is competent to be enumerated, it is competent to vote. If it is fit to have Representatives in Congress, and in the College of Electors, it is fit to take part in choosing them. It was always regarded by the free States as a sectional grievance that the South, under the Constitution as it was, had the right to count three-fifths of their slaves in determining the number of their Representatives in Congress and in the College of Presidential Electors. But it was submitted to because "so nominated in the bond." But now, after Slavery is destroyed, the South demand to be placed in even a more advantageous position than that which they then occupied, by insisting that the whites shall practically cast their votes for the whole, or, in other words, for five-fifths of their colored population, instead of but three-fifths as before; thus intending that the abolition of slavery shall inure largely to their benefit as an element of political power. This arrogant demand will not be conceded. This provision of the Constitution will stand as the supreme law, in spite of the maledictions of disunionists in the South or their allies in the North.

RECONSTRUCTION.

In the Summer of 1866, Congress tendered to the insurgent States this XIVth article, as the condition of their restoration to the Union. Pursuant to the evil counsels of the leaders in the Rebellion and an unwise President, they refused to accept it, and threw it back in the face of Congress and the people of the North. The elections of that year triumphantly sustained the XXXIXth Congress, and thereupon, in the closing hours of that body, and in the opening hours of its successor, a revised plan of reconstruction was proffered to the South, wherein the Rebel States were required, as condition precedent to their complete restoration to the Union, to ratify this XIVth article, and to adopt Constitutions that should confer the right of suffrage equally upon loyal whites and blacks. This plan has been fully accepted by seven of the ten late Rebel States, and is in advanced stages of completion in the remaining three. To this entire scheme the Democratic party has declared its implacable hostility, pronouncing these acts of Congress and the State Governments erected under them, to be " usurpations, and unconstitutional, revolutionary, and void ;" and by its candidate for Vice-President, and the utterances of its Southern leaders, has avowed its purpose to overthrow these Governments, deprive the loyal blacks of the elective franchise, and threatens to carry its hostility to the point of precipitating the country into another civil war.

In the face of such declarations, the question at issue is not whether this plan of reconstruction is the best that could have been devised, nor whether the loyal blacks are entitled to the ballot ; but it rather is, whether the authority of the Government shall be sustained and the Union maintained against the machinations and assaults of traitors who owe to the forbearance of the Government the very breath with which they now anathematize its laws and threaten its existence. But this provision of the reconstruction scheme will be sustained. Free suffrage is a Democratic principle, and will be maintained by a Democratic people, even though it be re-

pudiated by a party that has preserved nothing of Democracy
except the name.

"Right is right, since God is God,
And right the day shall win;
To doubt would be disloyalty,
To falter would be sin." [Cheers.]

These gentlemen who threaten to overthrow the reconstruction
policy by force, count without their host. Gov. Seymour is not
going to be elected, and one of the most powerful influences that
will contribute to his defeat is these very threats. A vast majority of the people North and South will not clothe with power
those whom they even suspect of a desire to reopen in any way,
and especially by an appeal to force, issues which have been settled amid the blaze and carnage of hundreds of battle-fields. They
will, through the ballot boxes, set the seal of their indignant repro-
bation upon a party that threatens to introduce into this Republic
that system of violence as a redress for real or fancied political
evils, which has so long cursed the Spanish-American States of
this Continent.

This experiment, once tried, has cost the Republic seven thou-
sand millions of money, and half a million of lives, and has
entailed upon us and our posterity a colossal debt, inexorable
taxation, and a long train of political, social, and financial calamities. The mass of our considerate and conservative citizens
have determined that this shall suffice for at least the remainder
of the present century, and they will not only withhold power
from, but will blot out of existence, the Democratic party, or any
party that attempts to reverse this irrevocable decree.

THE DEMOCRATIC PARTY.

In this connection, let me say, in justice to the Democratic
masses at the North, I believe them to be honest in their convictions,
and patriotic in their purposes, and that they will not long consent
to be led either by pardoned, yet unrepentant, Rebels of the South
or their allies at the North. The Democratic party was once the
champion of equal rights and universal suffrage, of progress and
reform. But through its affiliations with Slavery its brain became

palsied and its heart corrupted. It was by the Southern members of this party that the Rebellion was brought on. Their Northern associates opposed coercion, discouraged enlistments, opposed the draft, opposed the raising of money to carry on the war, opposed the abolition of Slavery even as a war measure. They were in favor of restoring the Rebel States without any safeguard for freedom, and would gladly have given back every slave to his master, and compelled the nation, tax-ridden as it is, to pay for every slave that was liberated, or let "the erring sisters depart in peace." Gov. Seymour, in a speech delivered by him to his fellow-townsmen of Utica, in October, 1861, said:

"If it is true that Slavery must be abolished to save the Union, then the people of the South should be allowed to withdraw themselves from the Government which cannot give them the protection guarranteed by its terms."

What is that but an explicit avowal that Slavery must be protected though the Republic perish. Compare these utterances with the noble sentiments of Gen. Grant, who, in reply to the Memphis Committee, said: "The only true foundation for human government is human liberty."

Fortunately for our country, the Democratic party, throughout its career, has been divided into two classes, the one clinging to the dead past, the other advancing toward the glowing future. They have differed, not merely upon questions of policy, but at various epochs have been found for and against the honor, the glory, the very existence, of the Republic. In remote days we saw Burr, the Democratic traitor, plotting to dismember the Union; and Jefferson, the founder of the Democratic party, bringing him into a court of justice, that he might be punished for his crimes.

Thirty-eight years ago, while John C. Calhoun, the author of Nullification and the father of Secession, was, in the name of Democracy, undermining the Republican fabric, Andrew Jackson uttered the talismanic sentiment: "The Federal Union! It must and shall be preserved!" At a later era, during the struggles over the application of the Wilmot Proviso in the Territories acquired in the Mexican war, when Foote of Mississippi, and King of Alabama, and other Democratic disciples of the Calhoun school of **Slavery** propagandists, threatened to dissolve the Union if this time-honored proviso were enforced; Benton, Wright, and Van Buren, whose names were the synonyms of Democracy, vindicated both the proviso and the Union. In the recent crisis of our Union we have seen Douglas and Dix, and Dickinson, and Holt, and Wadsworth, renowned Democratic chieftains, giving the best services, and some of them their heart's blood, to sustain a Government which Davis, and Breckinridge, and Toombs, and Cobb, and Wise, were fighting to destroy. And for the victory that awaits Ulysses S. Grant in November, himself a true Democrat, he will be largely indebted to Democrats who can distinguish between principles and professions, and prefer an honest creed to a sounding name. [Cheers.] Men who are ready to exclaim :

> " In your opinions look not always back ;
> Your wake is nothing, mind the coming track ;
> Leave what you've done, for what you have to do,
> Don't be consistent, but be simply true."   [Applause.]

" LET US HAVE PEACE."

Fellow citizens, this country needs repose. It has suffered under four years of sanguinary strife, followed by four years of political commotion. The foundations of our civil institutions have been shaken ; our trade, manufactures, agriculture, and industrial pursuits of all kinds have languished ; our financial affairs have been thrown into disorder ; the different departments of the Government have been brought into violent collision ; men's hearts have failed them through fear. Everything that is noble, and good, and generous in the land, cries out, " Let us have Peace." The people desire to see an end to this turbulent, vexatious, uncertain condition of things.

They know that the election of Grant and Colfax will bring them what their hearts so much covet—peace ! No sooner will the electric wires flash the news of their triumph over the Potomac and the Ohio, than that vast region, which for four years was scourged by war, and has since been the prey of passions hardly less ruinous than war, will lapse into a state of repose such as it has so much needed, but has not been able to enjoy for eight calamitous years. Partisan strife will then give way to peaceful

avocations. Interest in manufactures and agriculture will super-
sede the excitement of the caucus. The music of the mill will
silence the din of the hustings. The Common School will be more
respected than the political convention, and a lecture on practical
science will draw more hearers than the most fervid stump ha-
rangue. The South will then begin to see that an excess of politics has been her ruin, and will turn all her energies to building
up her waste places, developing her immense resources, reviving
her drooping industry, instructing the masses of her population,
and moving foward in a new career of prosperity and glory. In
a word, she will realize what the North fully comprehends, that
the cause for which she fought is irretrievably lost. Taught sub-
mission to the inevitable results of the war by bitter experience,
she will turn her back upon the gloomy past and open her eyes to
the bright future; and ere long become a powerful, rich, intelligent, and law-abiding section of the Union.

EFFECT OF SEYMOUR'S ELECTION.

But elect Seymour and Blair, and every hopeful feature of this
picture will be reversed. At once the South will commence a
crusade to upheave the work of reconstruction. She will struggle
to overthrow what she is pleased to call the carpet-bag government. She will aim to deprive the colored population of the suffrage. She will, in brief, do her utmost to retrieve the lost cause.
That her efforts in this direction will be measureably in vain, we
may well believe. For even should Gov. Seymour be elected, the
people who fought out the issues of the late war at the cost of so
much treasure and blood will not consent to see its fruits either
fraudulently or violently wrested from them.

Gov. Seymour's administration, even if backed by the House of
Representatives, would be confronted throughout its entire existence
by a majority of the Senate. It could not repeal an existing statute
nor enact a new law, nor place in power any officer from the Secre-
tary of State down, without the consent of that body. Practically, it
could not carry into effect any one of its cherished measures. But the
consequences of even an ineffectual struggle to restore the ancient
regime would be none the less pernicious to the business interests
of the country, and especially to those of the South. For four
years the attention of the Southern people would continue to be

diverted from their true interests, and devoted to political agitation. No greater calamity could befall that portion of the Union, than to see it turn aside from the work of reviving its prostrate industry, and plunge anew into the stormy sea of politics, whereon its prosperity, its honor, its power, have once suffered so terrible a shipwreck.

Its worst enemies could wish it no more dire calamities than are sure to overwhelm it if its people, under the lead of those architects of ruin, Hampton, Hill, Beauregard, Toombs, Wise, Forrest, and Vance, should, in the event of the election of Seymour and Blair, attempt to execute their threats of overthrowing the Congressional policy of reconstruction, and setting up in its place the institutions and the policies which prevailed previous to the Rebellion.

EFFECT OF GRANT'S ELECTION.

On the other hand, the election of Gen. Grant, while it would inspire confidence everywhere, would inaugurate a reign of peace, of order, of permanency, of prosperity in the South, while that of Gov. Seymour would revive and invigorate the epoch of strife, of instability, of ruin, such as has blighted and cursed thirteen States, and twelve millions of people during four years of war, followed by three years of collision between embittered factions. Nor would the contrast be hardly less striking in the Northern States than in the Southern. What our people want—our capitalists and laborers, our business men and producers, of all classes—is national repose, national stability, national confidence, administrative ability in national affairs. They long for the arrival of the hour when that stormy sea of armed rebellion, political contention, and financial uncertainty, on which they have been tossed for eight years, will sink to rest. Its wild waves, and fierce tempests, and lurid skies have affrighted the timid, vexed the enterprising, and thwarted the plans of the most prudent and sagacious.

The material interests and the business men, of every grade and class, from the proudest millionaire to the humblest workman, anxiously await the return of peace and public order throughout the land. They are weary of this din and clamor about reconstruction, State rights, a white man's government, negro suffrage, amnesty, and the like, and long for a stable government with a settled policy. And they believe that the administration of Gen. Grant, sustained by a patriotic and patient people, will in due time secure them this far more certainly than would that of Gov. Seymour, whose platform suggests, and insinuates, at least, repudiation and revolution, and whose administration would rally to its support all the turbulent and rebellious elements of one section of the Union, with much that is untrustworthy and unpatriotic in the other. In a word, if Seymour is elected, nothing can be permanently settled for four years at least, for his success would be a signal of commotion throughout the country, for acrimonious collision between different branches of the Government—culminating finally, perhaps, in civil war. Whereas, if Grant is elected, that very fact will almost instantly dispose of all important disturbing issues, by promptly bringing all departments of the Government into such harmonious coöperation as to insure quiet and stability, and inspire hope and confidence in every part of the Union.

When the friction of that complicated government machinery ceases to affright the public ear, the national credit will improve; hope will revive; men will take courage; business, both at the North and South, will spring to its feet, and move forward with elastic step; commerce will spread her moldering wings; manufacture will unchain her idle wheels; trade will unbolt her closed doors, and the merchant, the mechanic, the miner, and the agriculturist, will feel a new life throbbing through their veins. The cotton and rice plantations of the South will once more vie with the corn-fields of the West. The ingenious mechanics of the East will compete anew in generous rivalry with the enterprising miners of the West. The coal and the iron of Pennsylvania and Maryland will again seek the seaboard marts in company with the gold and silver of California and Nevada, and the hemp and wool of Kentucky and Ohio. The Atlantic ports will resume their trade with Europe in American bottoms, while the completed Pacific Railway, the wonder of an age that teems with great improvements, shall realize the dream of Columbus by opening the gates of the Orient from the west. Then that little rivulet of additional trade with China, arising out of our new and peculiar relations with her, will widen and deepen into a generous river. At the present time the largest ocean steamers in the world, running between California, Japan, and China, are unable, even now, before the completion of the Pacific Railroad, to carry the passengers and freight which are offered.

By the election of Seymour and Blair all this rising prosperity will be checked, because it is impossible to conduct great enterprises in an unsettled state of affairs.

Let us not forget that the prosperity of the country depends wholly upon the condition precedent that peace and stability reign throughout our borders. Obscure the horizon by turbulence, and especially overcast the sky with the dark clouds of civil war, and these visions of coming prosperity dissolve in impending night.

THE FINANCIAL ISSUES.

The financial questions involved in this contest, though often discussed, I cannot wholly overlook. Our public debt presses heavily upon the industry of the country. The taxes which necessarily flow therefrom lay their grasp, directly or indirectly, upon everything we eat, drink, wear, or use. These are grievous burdens. But they were incurred in a noble struggle to preserve the Republic. He who gazes not without solicitude, upon the colossal proportions of our great debt; he who submits, not wholly without repining, to the searching exactions of the tax-gatherer; the millionaire who liquidates his heavy annual assessment; the laborer who pays enhanced prices for everything he consumes, should all remember that these burdens were heaped upon them by a band of Democratic Rebels, who, after shedding an ocean of blood and ruining one-half of the Union, and plunging the other half into unprecedented financial disasters, are now clamoring for the election of Seymour and Blair, and threatening in the event of their triumph to involve the country in another war. The necessity of creating this debt and levying these taxes is therefore to be charged exclusively to the treason of the Southern Democracy. The loyal masses firmly met the issue. The resources of the country proved adequate to the great emergency. The citizens contributed of their substance to its treasury, and freely gave their blood to vindicate its flag. We triumphed; and as the blood shall be held in everlasting remembrance by our children and our children's children, so posterity will discharge the debt to the utmost farthing, according to the letter and spirit of the contract, in the money of the civilized world. Aye! the bonds will be paid, as will the greenbacks also, and both in the currency of Christendom. [Applause.]

As the gratitude of the nation will prove ample to canonize the sacred dust of its heroic dead, so will its resources and its integrity be found sufficient to keep faith with those who trusted it in a dark and perilous era. The Democratic press in commenting upon the result of the late elections, tauntingly remarked that the bloated foreign bondholders were rejoicing because it might enable them to realize 100 cents for what they paid only 40 cents. If through the crimes of our enemies the national credit was thus debased, let us rejoice that through the virtues of our friends it is gradually improving, and ere long will arrive at what we all somuch desire—specie payment.

Why should the credit of Massachusetts, whose 5 per cent. bonds are now selling in London at 85 cents be so much better than the credit of the United States, whose 6 per cent. bonds bring in the same market only 74 cents? It is because the people of Massachusetts have been a unit in upholding the credit of the Commonwealth beyond peradventure or the possibility of a doubt; while the validity of the national debt has been questioned, and our credit materially damaged, by the authoritative declarations of the Democratic party.

Nations, like individuals, must ever be mindful that credit is not only the basis of all great enterprises, but is the life of an industrial people. The financial disasters that would follow the success of the Democracy would affect our credit in all the markets of the world. Large amounts of our bonds are held in Europe. The holders already show signs of uneasiness because of the Democratic threats of practical repudiation.

The character of our people is on trial on every Exchange beyond the Atlantic. Not the bondholders and moneyed men only in foreign lands, but those who stood up firmly for the Union during the war, earnestly deprecate the success of Seymour, and anxiously desire the triumph of Grant, so that the honor and integrity of the nation, both financially and politically, may be vindicated. John Bright, the champion of freedom and equal rights in his native land, whose thrilling eloquence resounded in our defence during the darkest period of the conflict, now ardently hopes for our success in the present issue. Count de Gasparin, the author of that invaluable tribute to our country, issued during the gloomiest hours of our struggle, " The Uprising of a Great People," earnestly desires the election of Grant and Colfax. So also do those other champions of liberty, Edward Laboulaye and Henri Martin, the French historian. "You are right," says the latter, "in believing that we are warmly interested in your Presidential contest. The election of a *soi disant* Democrat would be a great calamity, but we have full confidence in the success of General Grant."

On the other hand, those Europeans, who are the supple tools of despotism, and who longed for the overthrow of the great Republic in our late conflict, as earnestly hope for the election of Seymour and Blair; so that through another civil war and the repudiation of our obligations, the cause of Democratic institutions may be put to hazard, and the credit of their brightest exemplar be foully tarnished.

SEYMOUR AND WAR—GRANT AND PEACE.

Fellow citizens, it is wise to contemplate the purposes avowed by our opponents in the event of their triumph. They intend to set aside the reconstruction policy of Congress (now nearly completed) by force of arms. Their starting point is that declaration engrafted into their National Platform by the pen of Gen. Wade Hampton, wherein they proclaim that the reconstruction acts and the State Governments erected under them are "usurpations, and unconstitutional, revolutionary, and void." Gen. Blair, in a letter written just previous to the assembling of the Convention, and which procured him its nomination for the Vice-Presidency, struck the key note of their intents in these significant words. He says: "It would be the duty of the President elect to declare those acts null and void, disperse the carpet-bag State Governments, allow the white people to reorganize their own governments, and elect Senators and Representatives." Nay, more. "We must have a President," he says, "who will trample into dust the usurpations of Congress, known as the Reconstruction acts."

Are those incendiary doctrines of the Democratic platform, and these revolutionary declarations of the Democratic candidate for the Vice-Presidency, mere empty sounds, signifying nothing? Immediately on the adjournment of the Tammany Convention, they were caught and re-echoed by all the leading orators of the Democratic party in the South, amid tumultuous cheers of excited assemblies. Hampton, Vance, Hill, Toombs, Semmes, Beauregard,

Forrest, and other leading ex-Rebels have reiterated them before applauding thousands, in every variety of phrase, in all the insurgent States.

The leading Democratic journals of the South—at Charleston, Savannah, Mobile, Atlanta, and the other great centres—have spread them before their readers, in every form of rhetoric known to the editorial pen. Need I trouble you with the reading of these speeches and articles? They have become to us "as familiar as household words." We at once recognize them as of like tenor and effect with those which issued from the same lips and the same pens eight years ago, in the dark and troubled night which preceded our civil war.

Does charity require, does prudence allow, that we regard these threats as mere idle gasconade? These men are too intelligent to believe, they know us too well to cherish, the delusion that they can by mere bravado bully and frighten those who trampled them down in the late war. No. They mean to carry into execution their teachings, provided they can fight to regain the lost cause under the protecting ægis of an administration elected to give full force and effect to the nullification doctrines of their national platform and the sanguinary intentions of the Blair letter, but which they do not dare even to threaten, under the administration of Grant and Colfax.

I am aware that it has recently been claimed by these Southern orators and editors, that the North has put too stringent a construction upon these revolutionary utterances. But there stands the record. We do not construe; we merely quote. We do not interpret; we merely read. We do not comment, but simply give the plain, unvarnished text. We cite the platform and the letter; we refer to the speeches and the editorials, without note or gloss. And we tell the 105 eminent Rebels who sat in the Tammany Convention, and framed its resolutions, and dictated its nominations, and their echoes and expounders North and South, that though they may have since discovered that their treasonable utterances have ruined their party, for this canvass at least, they cannot be allowed at this stage of the trial to change the issues.

I would fain believe that the sober second thought of these men, traitors should I not say, rather, daring and reckless as they are, will induce them to abandon a scheme so treasonable in its inception, so impossible of execution. We need hardly tell them that if the legal voters of this country elect Gen. Grant to the Presidency, they will see to it that he is regularly inaugurated, in spite of all the Rebels south of Mason and Dixon's line, and all their allies north of it. Once installed in the White House, the hero of Donelson, of Vicksburg, of Chattanooga, and of Appomattox, would not lack the purpose, the courage, the skill, nor the means, to crush utterly and forever this attempt to retrieve the lost cause by precipitating the country in another civil war.

The more serious, in fact the only danger would arise from the election of Seymour. The revolutionary programme of the platform, of the Blair letter, and of the speeches of the leading ex-rebels, could then be reduced to practice by erecting new governments in the ten Southern States, irrespective of the governments already existing there. The two classes of governments with their antagonized officials would soon come into violent collision, and the authority of President Seymour would be invoked, and would no doubt be employed to overthrow the existing governments—or, in the words of would-be Vice-President Blair, " to disperse the carpet-bag Government." And this would inaugurate civil war.

Forewarned by these threats, true policy calls upon the patriotic and conservative elements of the country to avert the calamities that would follow the success of the Democratic nominees by electing Grant and Colfax by a majority so overwhelming as to dissolve every doubt, and silence the faintest breath of clamor or dissent.

SCHUYLER COLFAX.

What candid man doubts that the country will be safe under their rule, and that their elevation to the Presidency and Vice-Presidency will be followed by a season of quiet and repose? Of Mr. Colfax's large experience, liberal principles, strict integrity, popular manners, and ample capacity to discharge the high trusts about to be committed to his keeping, I need not speak. He is everywhere known and beloved as a wise statesman and Christian gentleman.

GEN. GRANT—HIS CHARACTER AND OPINIONS.

Gen. Grant is one of those grand characters on which the pen of history loves to dwell. Tried in war and in peace, and tested by every vicissitude of fortune, he has proved equal to all emergencies. [Cheers.] Simple in his manners, modest in his utterances, clear-headed and generous-hearted, liberal and magnanimous, but firm and courageous, honest, sincere, and truthful, the enemy of fraud, duplicity, and cant, patient and cautious in conceiving his plans, and resolute and skillful in their execution, and possessing to an extraordinary degree that sagacity which enables one to judiciously select subordinates, and put "the right man in the right place," he will prove as wise in the Cabinet as he was heroic in the field. Gen. Grant is not a prejudiced partisan, nor versed in the crooked ways of professional politicians. But his varied services during the war ; the wide authority he has exercised in a semi-civil capacity since the downfall of the Rebellion ; his supervision of the difficult and delicate task of reconstructing a shattered Union, have shown that he has those mental traits and habitudes of mind that qualify men for the skillful administration of public affairs on the broadest theater. Belonging to that school of men of whom Monroe and Jackson and Taylor were lively types, he has given ample proof that he only needs the occurrence of opportunity and the pressure of duty, to so conduct the affairs of the nation, as to win a place among the purest and ablest statesmen who have filled the Presidential chair.

Though not trained to civil office, nor accustomed to address his fellow-citizens, either with the pen or from the platform, Gen. Grant has spoken, and his sentiments are of the noblest and most inspiring character. Five years ago he said to the people of Tennessee : " The stability of this Government and the unity of this nation depend solely on the cordial support and the earnest loyalty of the people."

In his letter to the President, protesting against the removal of the gallant Phil. Sheridan from the command of the Fifth Military District, he said : " This is a Republic where the will of the people is the law of the land. I beg that their voice may be heard."

In his address to the armies of the Union, at the close of the

Rebellion, among other thrilling sentiment, he gave the following: "By your patriotic devotion to your country in the hour of danger and alarm, your magnificent fighting, bravery, and endurance, you have maintained the supremacy of the Union, overthrown all armed opposition to the enforcement of the laws, and the proclamations forever abolishing slavery—the cause and pretext of the Rebellion—and opened the way to the rightful authorities to restore order and inaugurate peace on a permanent and enduring basis on every foot of American soil."

In his reply to the committee notifying him of his nomination at Chicago, he showed both his modesty and his regard for the popular will when he said: "If chosen to fill the high office for which you have selected me, I will give to its duties the same energy, the same spirit, and the same will, I have given to the performance of all duties which have devolved upon me heretofore. Whether I shall be able to perform those duties to your entire satisfaction, time will determine. You have truly said that I shall have no policy of my own to interpose against the will of the people."

And in his formal letter of acceptance he has given the keynote of his administration: "Peace, and universal prosperity, its sequence, with economy of administration, will lighten the burden of taxation, while it constantly reduces the national debt. Let us have peace."

CONCLUSION.

How grandly do these plain, undisguised and genuine Democratic opinions compare with the elaborate and evasive effusions of the loquacious Seymour, and the rash and revolutionary declarations of the vociferous Blair. Finally: assured of the triumph of a ticket, of which every patriotic American may feel justly proud, it only remains for us to see to it, that the Empire State bears an honorable part in this struggle by falling into line with the advancing column, and giving her electoral vote to the soldier and the statesman who has proved himself

"Patient of toil, serene amid alarms,
Inflexible of faith, invincible in arms."

[Loud applause.]

www.ingramcontent.com/pod-product-compliance
Lightning Source LLC
Chambersburg PA
CBHW021622290326
41931CB00047B/1445